WORLD WAR II
HISTORY'S DEADLIEST CONFLICT

SIGNIFICANT PEOPLE OF WORLD WAR II

NATALIE HYDE

Crabtree Publishing Company
www.crabtreebooks.com

Author: Natalie Hyde

Publishing plan research and development: Crabtree Publishing Company

Editors: Jackie Dell, Lynn Peppas

Proofreaders: Kelly Stern, Wendy Scavuzzo

Editorial services: Clarity Content Services

Production coordinator and prepress technician: Tammy McGarr

Print coordinator: Margaret Amy Salter

Series consultant: Fayaz Chagani

Cover design: Ken Wright

Design: David Montle

Photo Research: Linda Tanaka

Front cover: Shashin Shuho, HarryTruman, Adolf Hitler, Joseph Stalin, Sir Winston Churchill, Allied bombing on the German city of Cologne (background)

Title page: Yalta conference in 1945 with Winston Churchill, Franklin D. Roosevelt, and Joseph Stalin

Content page: The Distinguished Flying Cross medal award; Adolf Hitler, Nazi dictator of Germany

Photo Credits:

Cover: Wikimedia: The National Archives UK (bkgrd), Greta Kempton (middle), public domain (top left and right), Ephraim Stillberg (bottom left) Shutterstock: © Sergey Goryachev: (bottom right); Back cover: Wikimedia: public domain Title page National Archives UK/INF14-447C-543; p3t Canadian Forces/408 "Goose" Squadron Association, PD/ww2database; p4 Harry S. Truman Library & Museum; p5 Made for the Office of War Information/Library of Congress 1a35287; p7 Dept. of National Defence/Library and Archives Canada/PA-104436; p8 left (clockwise) PD/wikipedia, PD/Russia, PD/ww2database; p9tr Kitkatcrazy/en.wikipedia/CC 3.0, Bundesarchiv, Bild 102-10460/ Heinrich Hoffmann/CC-BY-SA; p10, 11 PD/wikipedia; p12t Office for Emergency Management/Office of War Information. Overseas Operations Branch. New York Office. News and Features Bureau/Presse Illustrationen Hoffmann/The US National Archives and Records Administration/540179, IWM/H 14250; p13 Released to Public Domain by photographer; p14t The US National Archives and Records Administration/536017, Library of Congress; p15 Franklin D. Roosevelt Presidential Library; p16t US Army, Library and Archives Canada/PA-063634; p17 US Gov; p18 Bundesarchiv, Bild 183-41636-0002/CC-BY-SA; p19 The US National Archives and Records Administration/535560; p20 US Marine Corps/US National Archives and Records Administration; p21 PD/Government of Japan; p22 Dept. of National Defence/Library and Archives Canada/PA-137013; p23 PD/wikipedia; p24 The US National Archives and Records Administration/535927; p25t PD/USA, Christopher J. Woods/Dept. of National Defence/ Library and Archives Canada; p27 Bundesarchiv, Bild 101I-337-0036-02A; p28 US Navy; p29 Hardy, Wilf (Wilfred) (20th century)/Private Collection/© Look and Learn/ Bridgeman Images; p30 US Gov; p31 US Navy Photograph 80-G-K-14025/US National Archives; p32t McGill University Library, Rare Books and Special Collections, Canadian War Poster Collection, Reference no. WP2.R16.F3, Nicholas Morant/Dept. of National Defence/Library and Archives Canada/PA-190248; p33 Canadian Forces/408 "Goose" Squadron Association; p34 Dept. of National Defence/Library and Archives Canada/PA-002792; p35 Devon S.A. (Flying Officer)/IWM/CH1406; p36 Dept. of National Defence/Library and Archives Canada/PA-006346; p37 IWM/ ART LD 5798; p38 Library of Congress/H261-9332; p39 US Army Intelligence and Security Command; p40 PD/UK Government/IWM/A23916; p41t US National Archives and Records Administration/80-G-279375, US National Archives USA C-5904; p42t Library and Archives Canada/PA-056818, IWM/8308-29; p43 Dept. of National Defence/Library and Archives Canada/E-80027; p44t The National Archives UK, bl US Gov, PD/wikipedia.

t=Top, bl=Bottom Left, br=Bottom Right

Library and Archives Canada Cataloguing in Publication

Hyde, Natalie, 1963-, author
Significant people of World War II / Natalie Hyde.

(World War II : history's deadliest conflict)
Includes index.
Issued in print and electronic formats.
ISBN 978-0-7787-2115-4 (bound).--ISBN 978-0-7787-2119-2 (paperback).--
ISBN 978-1-4271-1697-0 (pdf).--ISBN 978-1-4271-1693-2 (html)

1. World War, 1939-1945--Biography--Juvenile literature. I. Title.

D736.H94 2015 j940.53092'2 C2015-904380-8
C2015-904381-6

Library of Congress Cataloging-in-Publication Data

Hyde, Natalie, 1963-
Significant people of World War II / Natalie Hyde.
pages cm. -- (World War II: history's deadliest conflict)
Includes index.
ISBN 978-0-7787-2115-4 (reinforced library binding) --
ISBN 978-0-7787-2119-2 (pbk.) --
ISBN 978-1-4271-1697-0 (electronic pdf) --
ISBN 978-1-4271-1693-2 (electronic html)
1. World War, 1939-1945--Biography--Juvenile literature. I. Title.

D736.H93 2015
940.53092'2--dc23

2015023294

Crabtree Publishing Company

www.crabtreebooks.com 1-800-387-7650

Printed in Canada/112015/EF20150911

Published in Canada
Crabtree Publishing
616 Welland Ave.
St. Catharines, Ontario
L2M 5V6

Published in the United States
Crabtree Publishing
PMB 59051
350 Fifth Avenue, 59th Floor
New York, New York 10118

Published in the United Kingdom
Crabtree Publishing
Maritime House
Basin Road North, Hove
BN41 1WR

Published in Australia
Crabtree Publishing
3 Charles Street
Coburg North
VIC, 3058

CONTENTS

INTRODUCTION

A GLOBAL WAR THAT DIVIDED THE WORLD

World War II (1939–1945) was a time of great destruction. Cities, bridges, roads, and factories were bombed all over Europe and Asia. More than 60 million people were killed. It was also a time of invention. There was a need for bigger and better weapons, tanks, and planes. This led to new **technology**. Scientists raced to invent jet engines, missiles, and atomic bombs.

The countries fighting in World War II belonged to one of two sides, called the Axis and Allied forces or powers. Three main countries formed the Axis powers: Germany, Italy, and Japan. The leaders of these countries wanted to expand their territories. Germany wanted to control most of Europe. Italy wanted control over the Mediterranean area. And Japan wanted to expand into East Asia and the Pacific.

BELOW: *Many cities were bombed during WWII, leaving people without homes, stores, and schools.*

RIGHT: *Many people contributed to the war effort, including women who went to work in factories that produced war weaponry and supplies.*

At the start of the war, the Allied powers included Britain, France, and Poland. Soon after, they were joined by Canada, Australia, New Zealand, and South Africa. The Soviet Union joined the Allies after Germany broke the **pact** it had signed with the Soviet Union. Brazil, China, Denmark, Greece, Norway, the United States, and other countries joined later. Together the Allied countries called themselves the United Nations (UN). In 1945, the UN became an official organization and allowed other countries to join.

By 1942, decisions about the Allies' actions were controlled by "The Big Three." They were Britain, the Soviet Union, and the United States. When China joined, they became the "Four Policemen."

What Do You Know?

Key people in WWII usually held high ranks in the armed forces, such as

- Field Marshal—the highest rank in an army
- Admiral of the Fleet—the highest rank in a navy
- Brigadier General/Air Commodore—the highest rank in an air force
- Commander in Chief—an officer in charge of a major section of a country's armed forces
- Supreme Commander—the military officer commanding all forces on one side of a war

WWII Allies and Axis Powers

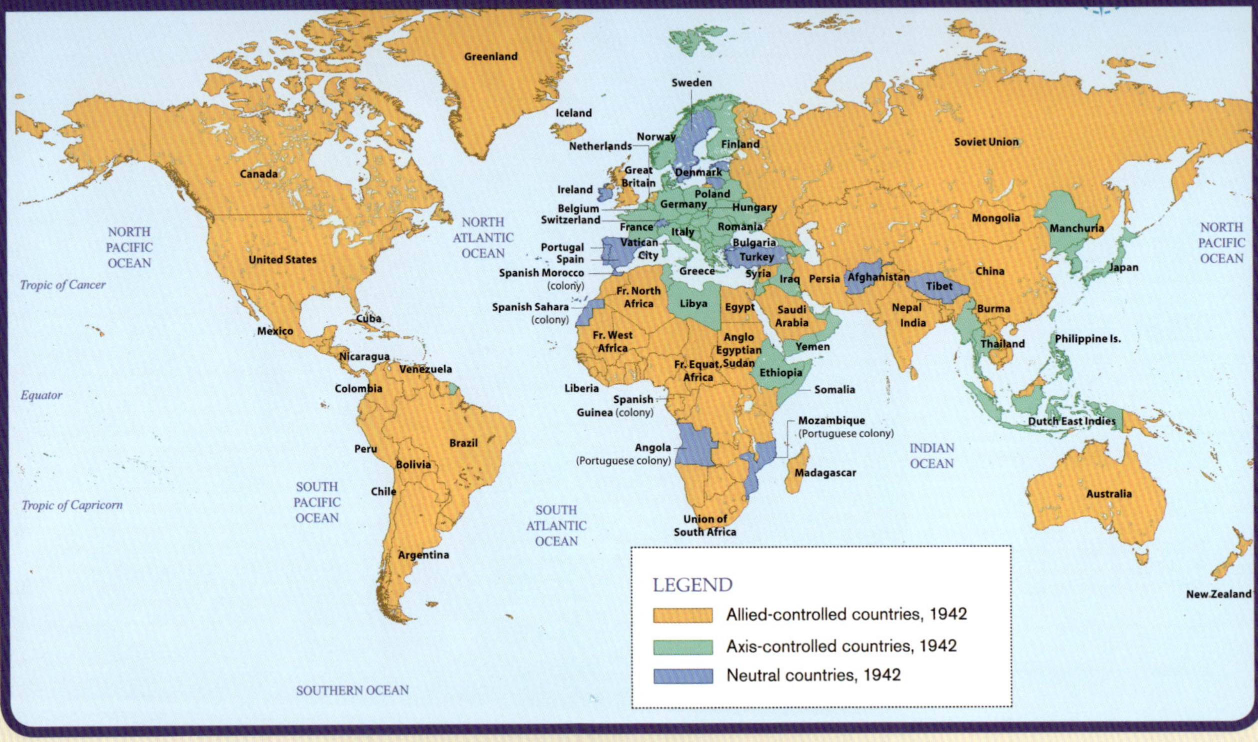

ABOVE: *Almost the entire world fought in WWII. This map shows all of the countries that were involved.*

By the end of 1942, almost every country in the world was involved in the war. Many countries wanted to avoid war. But the Japanese attack on the U.S. naval base at Pearl Harbor in Honolulu, Hawaii, brought even more countries into the fight.

The Axis was made up of only a few countries, which were also spread out. Those countries were powerful because of their leaders. Hitler (Germany), Mussolini (Italy), and Hirohito (Japan) were very **charismatic**. They convinced their citizens that war was necessary. They had also been preparing for war for a long time. Military leaders had already planned when and where they would attack.

It had only been 20 years since World War I. Many of the Allied countries hoped talks would prevent another conflict. The first few years after WWI were a time of hope and renewal for many countries. But by 1939, the world had fallen into an **economic** downturn. Many people were without jobs, homes, and even food. They turned to their leaders for solutions. When Hitler came to power, he made many changes. The German people credited him with turning the country around. They believed him when he said the limits put on Germany after WWI were unfair.

When the Axis powers declared war, Allied military leaders had to scramble to build up their forces. Most Allied countries had not prepared their troops. They had to quickly **recruit** and train new soldiers.

The heads of states made sure they had public support. They also had to keep people calm when things were bad. Without strong leadership, the Allies would not have been successful.

> ***What do you think?***
> **The Axis consisted of smaller and fewer countries. How did it become so powerful?**

BELOW: *The Allies had to train new soldiers to fight the Axis armies. These men are Canadian recruits learning to march.*

CHAPTER 1

AXIS STATESMEN IN WWII

The Axis began as an understanding between the chancellor of Germany, Adolf Hitler, and the prime minister of Italy, Benito Mussolini. They both wanted two things: to gain control over a large territory and to destroy **communism**. Japan had similar goals. On September 27, 1940, the three leaders signed the **Tripartite Act** and became known as the Axis Alliance.

Germany's Head of State: Adolf Hitler "Der Fuhrer" (The Leader)

When he was 25 years old, Hitler fought for Germany in World War I. He was decorated for bravery. When Germany **surrendered**, he was shocked. He felt let down by his country's leaders, and he found others in the German Workers' Party (**DAP**) who felt the same as he did. He became leader of the party in 1921. Eleven years later, he ran for president of Germany. He lost, but was named chancellor. He used this new position to form a **dictatorship**. Once he was dictator, he removed the president and declared himself the only leader. He also changed the name of the DAP to the Nazi Party and made it the only legal government party in Germany.

TOP: *Mussolini was the Fascist dictator of Italy.*

CENTER: *Stalin was the Communist leader of the Soviet Union.*

BOTTOM: *Hitler was the Nazi dictator of Germany.*

Hitler was a very powerful and passionate speaker. He created a "cult of personality." He did this by using the media, posters, and rallies to improve his image. He convinced the German people that he was a hero.

ABOVE: *The Nazis made every Jewish person wear a yellow fabric Star of David. They even made children wear them. The Nazis wanted to have an easy way to identify who was Jewish.*

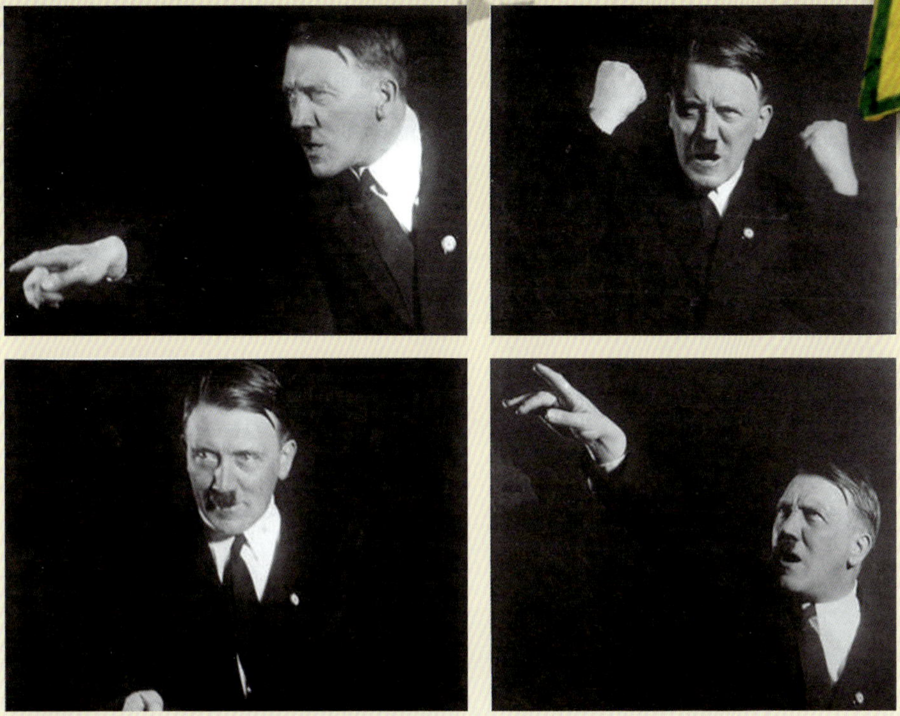

ABOVE: *Hitler was a great speaker, and he was able to make the German people excited about his plans.*

Hitler's dream was to create a master race of German people. He wanted to reclaim the land that he felt had been unfairly taken from them in previous wars. He blamed foreigners and Jewish people for Germany losing WWI, and for the economic problems in the country. He believed getting rid of Jews, foreigners, and other minorities would strengthen the nation. The Nazis killed 11 million people during the **Holocaust**.

Hitler was hiding underground in Berlin when he finally accepted that he had been defeated. Instead of facing trial for his war crimes, he committed suicide by taking a **cyanide** capsule.

What Do You Know?

While working for the DAP, Hitler was asked to design its banner. He created the infamous image of a black swastika in a white circle on a red background.

Italy's Head of State: Benito Mussolini, "Il Duce" (The Chief)

ABOVE: *Mussolini walks past enthusiastic young supporters of Fascism.*

Fascism is a type of government in which the nation is seen as more important than its individuals. Strict rules limit people's actions and punish those who act or speak against the government. It is run by a dictator who has total control. Benito Mussolini founded Italy's National Fascist Party in 1919. In 1922, he was elected president of Italy. By 1925, he had turned Italy into a dictatorship.

Mussolini wanted Italy to become a new Roman Empire. He began invading regions around Italy. He planned to take land from the Slavic people of Yugoslavia. He called them **barbarians**. He believed Italians were a superior people and deserved to take over other countries.

Mussolini signed a treaty of friendship with Hitler in October 1936, forming the Rome-Berlin Axis. Like Hitler, Mussolini was very charismatic and he also created a cult of personality. He hid his health problems from the public so that he would appear more powerful. He convinced Italians that he was a savior for the country. The people supported him when he declared war on France on June 10, 1940, and on the United States on December 11, 1941. He used his power to commit war crimes. His army used chemical weapons when it invaded Ethiopia. He also participated in Hitler's Holocaust. In 1945, he was arrested and **executed** by a **firing squad**.

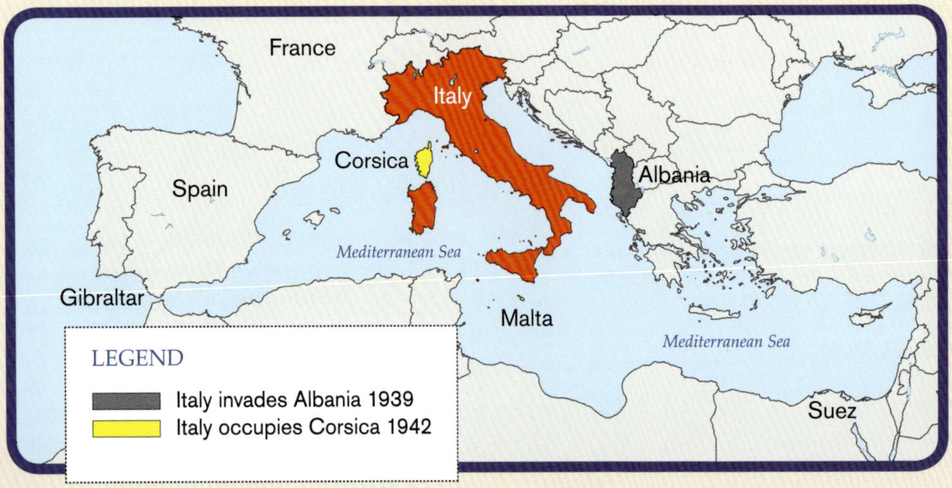

LEFT: *Mussolini invaded other countries because he wanted Italy to have an empire, the way it did under the ancient Romans.*

Japan's Head of State: Emperor Shōwa (Hirohito)

Michinomiya Hirohito became emperor of Japan in 1926, after the death of his father. Japan had become overcrowded, and the government had been looking west for more land. The Chinese region of Manchuria was large, and rich in minerals, forests, and farmland. When Hirohito's military leaders suggested invading Manchuria, he agreed. Japan began to build an army and invaded China in 1931. War broke out.

In 1940, Hirohito signed the Tripartite Act and joined the Axis powers of Germany and Italy. Japan made a surprise attack on Pearl Harbor in the United States in 1941. Months after WWII ended in Europe, the United States dropped two atomic bombs on Japan. The destruction and human loss was devastating. When the U.S. threatened further action, the Japanese Army wanted to continue fighting, but Hirohito urged peace. He made a radio broadcast on August 15, 1945, during which he announced Japan's surrender. Most of his power was then stripped away, and Japan became a **democracy**. Hirohito did not have to face war crime trials. Instead, he was forced into a lesser role of **figurehead**.

ABOVE: *Emperor Hirohito and Empress Kojun of Japan lived a very privileged life.*

Japan's Prime Minister: Hideki Tojo

In 1941, Emperor Hirohito named Hideki Tojo prime minister of Japan. As prime minister, Tojo ordered a surprise attack on the U.S. naval base in Hawaii. After the attack on Pearl Harbor, Tojo believed that Japan was winning the war. Then the United States began bombing **raids** on Japan, which caused a lot of damage and deaths. Emperor Hirohito thought Tojo was losing control. Tojo felt as though he had let Hirohito down, so he resigned as prime minister in 1944. After the war, he was tried for war crimes and was executed.

CHAPTER 2

ALLIED STATESMEN IN WWII

ABOVE: *Germany invaded France, but the Allies kept fighting.*

In 1939, Britain and France realized that Germany was a threat to peace in Europe. They began to prepare for war. After France fell to Germany, Britain continued to fight. It had the help of Canada and other **Commonwealth** countries. The Soviet Union and the United States joined the Allied forces later.

Britain's Head of State: Winston Churchill

Winston Churchill was 65 when he became prime minister in 1940, and he had held many political and cabinet positions in previous British governments. He was **First Lord of the Admiralty** from 1911 to 1915. During WWI, he served as a lieutenant colonel of an infantry battalion on the Western Front in France. In 1939, Winston Churchill was appointed First Lord of the Admiralty again. He also became a member of the War Cabinet. He saw Hitler as a huge threat to peace. Months before WWII began, Churchill urged his country to rearm. But Prime Minister Neville Chamberlain disagreed. Chamberlain upheld a policy of **appeasement** in an effort to prevent war. But on September 1, 1939, Germany invaded Poland. Days later, Allied countries declared war on Germany, and WWII began. British citizens realized Chamberlain's error and saw him as

ABOVE: *Churchill inspired the people of Britain through his bravery and determination to "never surrender."*

a weak leader. He resigned in May 1940. Churchill became Britain's prime minister a month later.

Churchill had a strong belief in democratic freedom and he had the ability to inspire the British people with his strong speeches. Many of his inspirational phrases are still used today.

As the war dragged on, Churchill proposed forming the "Grand Alliance." This was an agreement between the United States, the Soviet Union, and Britain to join forces to defeat the threat of Nazi Germany. The agreement was signed on June 22, 1941. The three countries became known as "The Big Three." The three countries had very different political systems, but they all recognized that they needed to work together to defeat the Axis powers.

Churchill is considered one of the greatest wartime leaders of the 20th century because of his strategic insights, passion, and personality.

The Soviet Union's Head of State: Joseph Stalin

Joseph Stalin was the Communist dictator of the Soviet Union from 1929 to 1953. At the beginning of WWII, Stalin and Hitler signed a Non-Aggression Pact that promised neither country would attack the other. In 1941, Hitler broke the pact when his army invaded the Soviet Union. Stalin then joined the Allies to fight against the Axis powers.

Using statues, paintings, and the media, Stalin built a cult of personality. The Allies in the West needed Stalin to defeat Hitler, but they didn't really trust him. Stalin ruled by terrorizing the Russian people. He caused a famine within his country and executed anyone who went against him. His **brutal** "reign of terror" caused the deaths of millions of his own people. Even after the war, Stalin continued his "reign of terror."

LEFT: *Stalin used many things such as statues and paintings to show people that he was a good leader.*

PRIMARY SOURCES

"...we shall fight on the landing grounds, we shall fight in the fields and in the streets, we shall fight in the hills; we shall never surrender."

—WINSTON CHURCHILL, JUNE 4, 1940

United States' Head of State: Franklin D. Roosevelt

When WWII broke out, Franklin Roosevelt was the president of the United States. Roosevelt provided supplies to both Britain and the Soviet Union. U.S. Navy ships protected Allied ships across the Atlantic Ocean, as far as Great Britain.

In the beginning, the American public was against joining the war. But after Japan attacked Pearl Harbor, Roosevelt called for war with Japan in his famous "Infamy Speech," and the anti-war feeling of the public vanished.

Japanese Americans living in the United States, some of whom were second-generation Americans, were treated like enemies. They were kept in **internment** camps. Later German Americans, and Italian Americans who were not citizens were also interned.

Roosevelt met with Churchill and Stalin many times to discuss **strategy**. Roosevelt planned to build the world's first atomic bomb. The name of the top-secret plan was "The Manhattan Project," but Roosevelt died before any bombs were tested or used.

BELOW: *During the war, even though they were American citizens, Japanese people were forced to live in internment camps such as this one at Tulelake, California.*

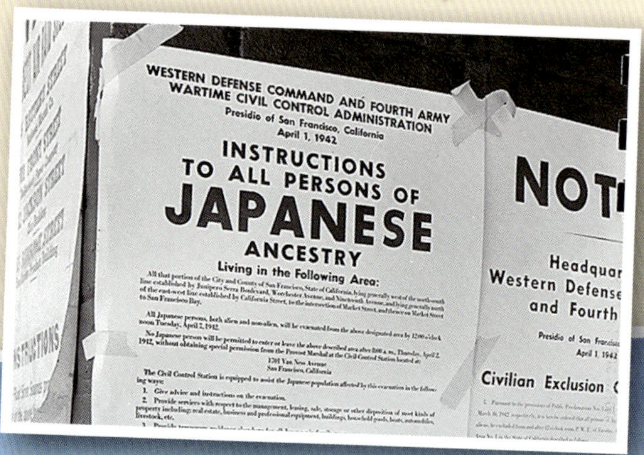

United States' First Lady: Eleanor Roosevelt

The First Lady of the United States, Eleanor Roosevelt, was one of the most outspoken women who had ever lived in the White House. She fought for black civil rights, human rights, and women's issues. When WWII broke out, she was against interning Japanese Americans. She was frustrated that she couldn't change President Roosevelt's mind. So she worked to make sure families were at least kept together in the camps.

Eleanor Roosevelt saw what was happening to Jewish people in Europe. She wanted to help Jewish children **emigrate** to the United States. She also supported having women replace men in the workplace while the men were at war. She set up training programs and programs to provide day care and equal pay for women.

ABOVE: *Eleanor Roosevelt cared a lot about what was happening to families in the United States during the war.*

United States' Head of State: Harry S. Truman

When Franklin D. Roosevelt died in 1945, Vice President Harry S. Truman became president of the United States. Truman took over during a difficult time. The Allies had achieved victory in Europe, but the war with Japan dragged on. Truman was told about a newly available weapon—the atomic bomb. He had to decide whether to use it. Truman and his advisers agreed that to end the war and save lives, they would need to use atomic bombs. A few days after the bombings, Japan surrendered.

PRIMARY SOURCES

"I knew what I was doing when I stopped the war that would have killed a half a million youngsters on both sides if those bombs had not been dropped. I have no regrets and, under the same circumstances, I would do it again."

—HARRY S. TRUMAN, AUGUST 5, 1963

LEFT: *Charles de Gaulle, on the left, led the French resistance to German occupation while he was in London.*

France's Head of State: Charles de Gaulle

In 1940, the Nazis defeated France. France signed an agreement giving Germany the right to **occupy** northern and western France. Charles de Gaulle was an officer in the French army who refused to accept the agreement. He gave a speech on June 18, 1940, urging the French to continue fighting the Axis powers.

De Gaulle became the leader of the Free French— a government that was set up in and operated out of London, England. He supported French Resistance movements in France that consisted of men and women determined to keep fighting against the Nazis. They also helped trapped Allied soldiers and pilots escape. After the war ended, de Gaulle became leader of the new French Republic.

Canada's Head of State: William Lyon Mackenzie King

William Lyon Mackenzie King was the prime minister of Canada during WWII. He declared war one week after Chamberlain did to show Canada's independence from Great Britain. Canadian troops were sent to fight in Italy, Germany, and France. King wanted a strong Canadian military, so he built up the Royal Canadian Air Force (RCAF). King worked with other Commonwealth countries to create the British Commonwealth Air Training Plan (BCATP). This Canadian program prepared more than 200,000 people for the Allied air forces. After the bombing of Pearl Harbor, King bowed to public pressure and interned Japanese Canadians in camps, like the United States government was doing.

BELOW: *King's BCATP was a major factor in the success of the Allied air forces in WWII.*

What Do You Know?

The Tuskegee Airmen were the first African-American pilots in the U.S. Armed Forces. African-Americans were not allowed to fight alongside whites during WWII. They were part of all-black units. There were 996 pilots who flew more than 15,000 missions. Their success earned them a lot of respect, and their work paved the way for **integrated** units.

BELOW: *The Tuskegee Airmen, through their skill and dedication, proved that blacks and whites could be in the same fighting units.*

Newfoundland's Head of State

Newfoundland was not part of Canada during World War II. It was a British **dominion**. But Newfoundlanders were some of the first to volunteer to fight. The governor of Newfoundland was Sir Humphrey Thomas Walwyn. He encouraged Newfoundlanders to join the war effort. Newfoundlanders provided lumber, food, and other supplies for the Allies. More than 22,000 men and women joined units in Britain and in other countries.

CHAPTER 3

KEY MILITARY LEADERS AND SOLDIERS IN WWII

Military leaders during WWII were responsible for the movement of troops, ships, and planes. Decisions about when and where to fight changed as they got new information. Each side was always trying to stay one step ahead of the other.

KEY AXIS MILITARY LEADERS IN WWII

The men leading the Axis forces had spent their lives in the military. They were ruthless and daring commanders. They developed new war strategies and weapons to try to lead the Axis to victory.

Nazi Military Leaders in WWII

The armed forces of Germany were called the *Wehrmacht*. Its weapons, fighting methods, speed, and brutality made it a powerful force.

Heinrich Himmler

Himmler was the leader of the Nazi SS (*Schutzstaffel*: Protection Squad). He was the second most powerful man in Germany, after Hitler. He had two major responsibilities: He was in charge of security inside the country, and he also oversaw Hitler's plan for a pure race of Germans.

RIGHT: *The Nazi SS were in charge of security inside Germany. They were known as the "secret police" and were feared by most people.*

LEFT: *Prisoners died of malnourishment, disease, starvation, and murder in Nazi death camps like this one called Buchenwald.*

Himmler's plan for racial purity was called the "Final Solution." He set up the first **death camp** at Dachau. By the end of the war, there were almost 50 such camps. When Himmler realized that Germany was losing the war, he tried to hide by shaving his mustache and fleeing. He was caught and handed over to the British. Instead of facing trial, he killed himself by taking a cyanide capsule.

Erwin Rommel

Rommel was Hitler's favorite general. He was in charge of the *Blitzkrieg* (lightning war) in northern Europe. This type of war **tactic** used a combination of tanks, air power, and soldiers, moving very quickly to attack. Rommel used this technique to invade Belgium, Netherlands, and France.

After his success in France, Rommel was sent to head the German forces in Africa. He was a master of desert warfare. There he earned the nickname "Desert Fox." He was considered a humane officer and ignored orders to kill Jewish soldiers. He was never accused of any war crimes.

Rommel did not agree with many of Hitler's plans. When he returned to Germany, he helped with a plot to kill Hitler that involved bombing one of his meetings. The plot failed. Hitler suspected that Rommel was involved in the plan. Because Rommel was so well liked, Hitler didn't want to risk looking bad by killing him. So he persuaded Rommel to commit suicide. Hitler promised that if he did, Rommel's family would not be harmed.

What do you think?

Why was Heinrich Himmler one of the most feared men in Nazi Germany?

Japanese Military Leaders in WWII

The Imperial Japanese Army was formed after the shoguns were defeated. Shoguns were **feudal** lords who had their own soldiers. The new Imperial Army was loyal only to the emperor. This loyalty included dying a "glorious death" (*gyokusai*) instead of **surrendering** or being taken prisoner.

Tomoyuki Yamashita

Yamashita was the lieutenant general of the Imperial Japanese Army. In 1940, he met with Hitler and Mussolini. The next year, Yamashita led the attack on Malaya and Singapore, where he defeated the British and Commonwealth forces.

The Japanese Army captured the largest number of British prisoners of war (POWs) in military history. The victory earned Yamashita the nickname "Tiger of Malaya."

After this victory, Yamashita's troops committed terrible crimes against POWs and civilians. These crimes were used as evidence in Yamashita's war crimes trial. He claimed he did not know what his troops were doing. In the end, he was still found guilty and hanged. This trial was used as an example to show that officers are held responsible for the actions of their troops. Being responsible for their troops was declared to be an officer's duty, even if they did not know what was happening or were unable to stop it. It was called the "Yamashita Standard" and it helped convict other officers of war crimes.

Masaharu Homma

Homma was a general in the Imperial Japanese Army. He led the **invasion** and capture of the Philippines in 1941. His troops held more than 60,000 POWs. Homma was in charge of the Bataan Death March. The March began on April 9, 1942, when Japanese troops forced the POWs to walk more than 64 miles (100 km) to a new camp. More than 21,000 POWs died along the way. This event was included in the list of Homma's war crimes. He was executed in 1946 as a war criminal.

BELOW: *Many soldiers died on the Bataan Death March. The March was considered a war crime.*

What Do You Know?

Second Lieutenant Hiroo Onoda took his orders seriously to not surrender and not be taken prisoner. When WWII ended, he was hiding on an island in the Philippines. He did not lay down his weapons until his former commander came to the island to relieve him of his duties…almost 30 years later.

Three decades after the war ended, soldier Hiroo Onoda of the Japanese Army was still on duty.

PRIMARY SOURCES

> "Lieutenant Onoda, sir, reporting for orders."
>
> —HIROO ONODA, UPON MEETING HIS SUPERIOR, TANIGUCHI, AFTER 30 YEARS OF HIDING

KEY ALLIED MILITARY LEADERS IN WWII

The Allied leaders had to deal with changes in warfare. New weapons and technology forced them to adapt quickly to succeed.

American Military Leaders in WWII

The attack on Pearl Harbor, which brought the United States into the war, was unexpected. Military leaders had to work quickly to make their battle plans. The armed forces were not at their peak strength. Leaders had to get troops trained and ready to fight.

BELOW: *Allied troops landing on D-Day at Juno Beach in Normandy, France*

George Marshall

Marshall became chief of staff of the U.S. Army the day the war started in Europe. At that time, the army was quite small. It would have easily been crushed by Hitler's *Wehrmacht*. But by 1942, Marshall had worked to build the forces to more than eight million well-trained soldiers and officers. General Marshall also helped to organize "Operation Overlord"—the code name for the Allied invasion of Europe.

After the war, Marshall created a plan to help Europe recover. The Marshall Plan helped Europe modernize its industries and get rid of **trade barriers**. In 1953, Marshall received a Nobel Peace Prize for his work.

Douglas MacArthur

MacArthur was an experienced WWI soldier. In 1930, he was promoted to general. MacArthur was posted to the Philippines in 1941. The day after the attack on Pearl Harbor, the Japanese attacked MacArthur's troops. His air force was destroyed. But his troops were rescued, and he vowed to return. In 1944, he released the Philippines from Japan's control. On September 2, 1945, MacArthur accepted Japan's surrender aboard the USS *Missouri*.

Dwight Eisenhower

Eisenhower was the Supreme Commander of the Allied forces in Europe. He planned and supervised the attack in North Africa. He also led the invasion of Europe that began on **D-Day**—June 6, 1944. After the war, he was named Supreme Allied Commander of the North Atlantic Treaty Organization (**NATO**). In 1952, he was elected the 34th president of the United States.

George Patton

General Patton was a fearless military leader. During the D-Day invasion, his troops swept across France. In 1945, he continued across the Rhine River and into Germany. He freed much of Germany from the Nazis. He was called "Old Blood and Guts" because of his passion for battle.

What do you think?

If you had to create a recovery plan for Europe after the war, what would it include?

BELOW: *General Patton was widely admired by the troops he commanded.*

British Military Leaders in WWII

Before WWII, the British army was small, not well equipped, and no match for the larger, more advanced *Wehrmacht*. After war was declared, Britain used **conscription** to bring in more troops. By 1945, more than 3.5 million men and women had served in the armed forces.

BELOW: *Montgomery led his troops to victory over the Nazis in North Africa.*

Bernard Montgomery

Major General Montgomery was given command of the Eighth Army in North Africa. He defeated Rommel and the Nazis at El Alamein, Egypt. This victory turned the tide of the war. On D-Day, Montgomery led the British and Canadian forces in Normandy, France. His troops took over the port of Antwerp in Belgium. He accepted the formal surrender of the Germany military on May 4, 1945.

Canadian Military Leaders in WWII

Canada was the first Commonwealth country to send troops to Britain in 1939. More than 40 percent of men between the ages of 18 and 45 enlisted voluntarily. The German army respected the Canadians. From their experience fighting the Canadians in WWI, the Germans knew that they were expert and professional soldiers.

Andrew McNaughton

General McNaughton was a scientist, engineer, and military officer. During WWII, he was the commander of the First Canadian Infantry Division. He believed in men volunteering to fight rather than the government using conscription. He helped design **ammunition** that could break through the metal coating of tanks and guns. He was also part of the raid on the port of Dieppe. That battle was a disaster, and many lives were lost. McNaughton took much of the blame for the failure.

THOMAS (TOMMY) PRINCE

Tommy Prince was a member of the Brokenhead Ojibway Nation in Manitoba. He became a member of the First Special Service Force, and spied on the Germans in Italy. One day, a shell broke his communication wire. Dressed as a farmer, he walked into the field where the cable was. He pretended to tie his shoe, then repaired the cable in full view of the German soldiers. His bravery earned him many medals. He is Canada's most decorated Aboriginal war veteran.

ABOVE: *Tommy Prince, pictured on the right, with his brother at Tommy's award ceremony at Buckingham Palace in 1945.*

CHAPTER 4

KEY AIR FORCE LEADERS AND PILOTS IN WWII

Air warfare played a big role in WWII. Both sides used their planes to disrupt supplies and support troops on the ground. They knew that a powerful air force could help win the war.

KEY AXIS AIR FORCE LEADERS AND PILOTS

At the beginning of World War II, the Axis powers had a strong air force. They had been preparing for war longer than the Allies. They had better equipment, and their pilots were better trained. As the war dragged on, new technology allowed the Allies to improve their skills and even beat the Axis powers in the air.

Germany's Air Force Leaders and Pilots

The *Luftwaffe* was Germany's air force. After WWI, the German air force was shut down. However, German pilots trained in secret. At the beginning of WWII, the *Luftwaffe* was one of the most advanced air forces in the world. Its fighter plane was called the *Messerschmitt*. These planes caused great damage to Britain during the *Blitzkrieg*.

Hermann Goering

Goering was famous in Germany as a World War I fighter **ace**. After WWI, he joined the Nazi Party. Goering formed the Nazi secret police—the *Gestapo*—in 1933. In 1935 Hitler gave Goering command of the *Luftwaffe*. After WWII had ended in Europe, Goering was convicted and given the death sentence for war crimes and crimes against humanity at the **Nuremberg trials** for the part he played in the Holocaust. He committed suicide the night before he was supposed to be hanged.

OPPOSITE PAGE: *German pilots with the* Messerschmitt*—the most modern bomber plane of its time.*

The *Blitzkrieg* on Poland gave Germany a quick victory. Goering targeted Britain next. The Germans needed to control the English Channel. To do this, they needed to defeat the British air force. The British had the advantage of **radar**. They could see where the German fighters and bombers were, and how many were coming. Goering did not fully understand the importance of radar, so he did not order all radar stations to be bombed. This mistake helped the Allies defeat the Germans in the air.

Albert Kesselring

Kesselring was known as "Uncle Albert" to his troops. He commanded German air forces in Poland and France. He was shot down five times during WWII, but survived. Later, Kesselring transferred to Italy. There, he was overall commander of the German forces in the Mediterranean and North Africa. He used air support to back up Rommel's troops on the ground in North Africa. He was tried for war crimes after the war and found guilty. His death sentence was later changed to life imprisonment. He was released from prison in 1952 because of his bad health, and died in 1960.

What Do You Know?

Erich Hartmann is considered the highest scoring ace of all time. He shot down 352 planes in his *Messerschmitt*.

ABOVE: *Japanese air crew preparing fighter planes for battle on the Japanese aircraft carrier* Shokaku.

Japan's Air Force Leaders and Pilots

The main job of the Imperial Japanese Air Force was to support ground forces. Pilots would delay, disrupt, or destroy the army or the enemy's supplies. The Japanese "Zero" fighter planes were feared during **dogfights**. They moved quickly and could fly long distances.

Takijiro Onishi

In WWII, Onishi was in command of the Japanese Navy Air Service, which was a branch of the military that dealt with aircraft carriers. These huge ships could carry and launch planes. This made air attacks in distant places possible.

ABOVE: *A Japanese* **kamikaze** *is flying his plane toward an Allied ship.*

In 1944, Onishi was ordered to attack Allied aircraft carriers in the Pacific. He ordered his pilots to fly suicide missions. These pilots crashed their planes into the ships, killing themselves. These ***kamikaze*** pilots were told their fighting spirit would keep Japan from defeat.

Saburo Sakai

Fighter pilot Sakai was a flying ace of the Imperial Japanese Navy. Sakai claimed to have shot down more than 60 planes during the war.

Sakai was wounded in a dogfight near the Solomon Islands in the Pacific Ocean. A bullet struck him in the head and right eye. Badly wounded, he managed to pull his plane out of a dive into the ocean and made it back to his base. He never recovered his full vision, but he returned to duty near the end of the war. After the war, he became a Buddhist and vowed never to kill another living thing.

Hiroyoshi Nishizawa

Nishizawa was called "the Devil" when he was flying. He often found enemy planes before anyone else could see them coming.

After downing more than 80 planes, he was promoted and became a trainer, but Nishizawa didn't like it. He wanted to fly missions but was posted to the Philippines, where he realized that Japan was losing the war. He volunteered to become a *kamikaze* pilot, but was turned down. As he flew back to Japan on a transport plane, it was shot down and Nishizawa died.

PRIMARY SOURCES

"Never have I seen a man with a fighter plane do what Nishizawa would do with his Zero. His aerobatics were all at once breathtaking, brilliant, totally unpredictable, impossible, and heart-stirring to witness."

—SABURO SAKAI, ABOUT HIS FRIEND HIROYOSHI NISHIZAWA

KEY ALLIED AIR FORCE LEADERS AND PILOTS

The Allied air forces worked together to win the battle of the skies. They had command of the air space over the Pacific in 1943, and Europe in 1944. This meant that supplies could get to Allied troops but not to Axis forces. It also meant the Allies could attack enemy lines and cause great damage.

ABOVE: *A group of Allied B-52 planes fly towards their targets.*

The United States Army Air Force Leaders and Pilots

When war broke out in 1939, the U.S. Air Force was not ready to fight. Their planes were not advanced enough to take on the *Luftwaffe*. After the Pearl Harbor attack, the Army Air Force (AAF) was created. More advanced planes were built and more pilots were trained. By the end of the war, the AAF **dominated** the skies over Europe and Japan.

George Churchill Kenney

In 1942, General Kenney was assigned to be General MacArthur's air commander. Kenney was the first to use skip bombing. This was a special method in which bomber pilots flew very low and released the bombs so that they skipped across the water, like stones on a pond. Kenney's methods and strategies resulted in many victories for the Allies. Kenney joined MacArthur aboard the USS *Missouri* for the Japanese surrender.

James H. Doolittle

Before WWII, Doolittle was a test pilot. Four months after the attack on Pearl Harbor, Doolittle was asked to perform a special mission. He was to lead a **raid** on Tokyo, Japan. Sixteen B-25 bombers took off from an aircraft carrier in the Pacific, and dropped their bombs on industrial and military targets. These planes were too big to land on the carrier, so they flew on to China. The bombers ran out of fuel and had to crash land. Most of the crew members parachuted to the ground and made it safely back to the American lines. The Doolittle Raid did a lot to lift the spirits of Americans.

John Thach

Thach was a pilot who developed the Thach Weave. It was a way for the slower-moving American jets to win against the faster-turning Japanese Zeros. Two pilots would weave back and forth as they flew. The enemy would be forced to come into range as he tried to follow them. The Thach Weave was used during the Battle of Midway. It was so successful that it was used many times after.

BELOW: *The Allies successfully used the Thach Weave during the Battle of Midway.*

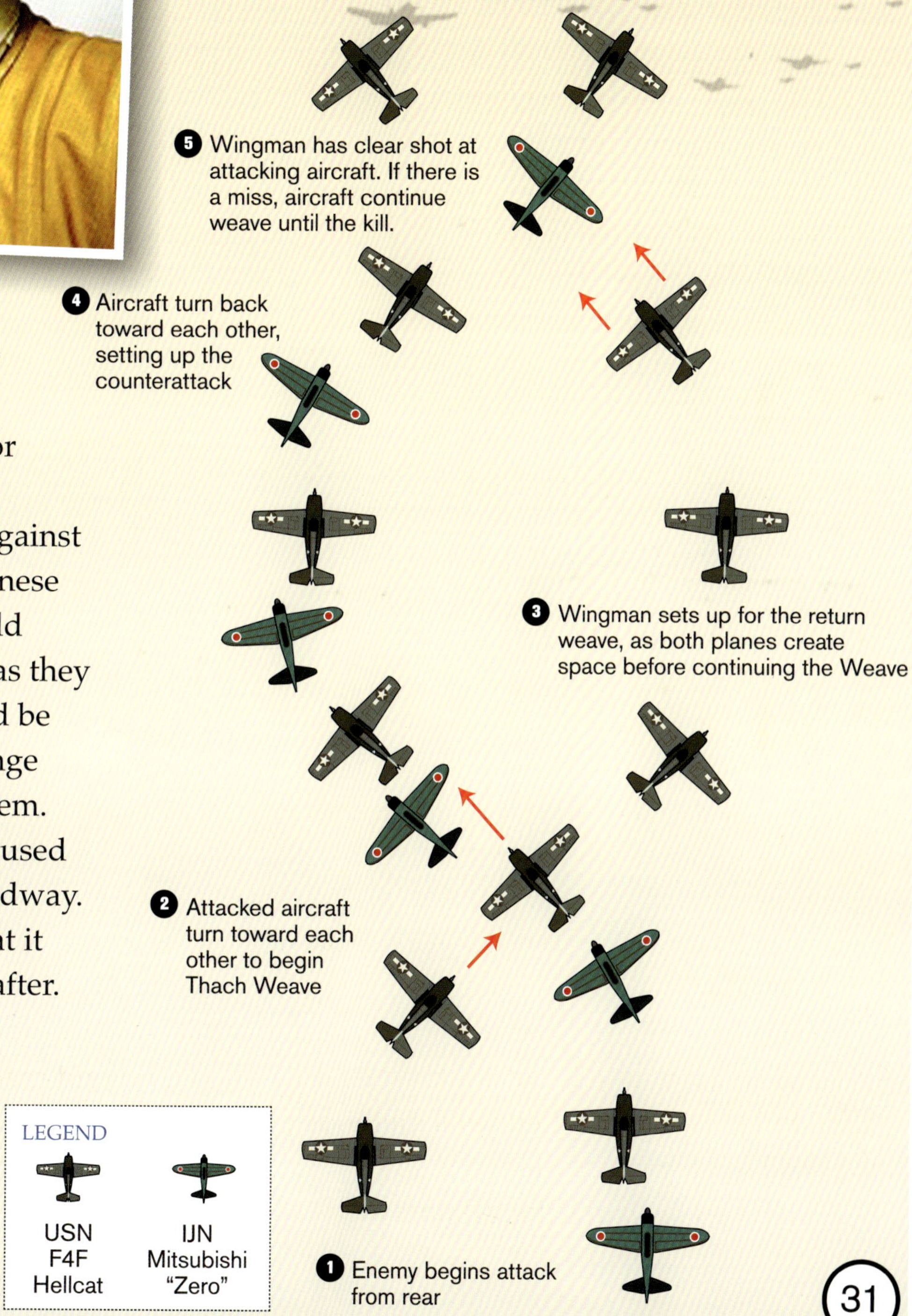

The Royal Canadian Air Force Leaders and Pilots

In the first month of WWII, the Royal Canadian Air Force (RCAF) only had about 29 planes to use in battle. But by 1944, the RCAF was the fourth-largest Allied air force. Its success was due in part to the British Commonwealth Air Training Plan. The BCATP was developed from an agreement between Canada, the United Kingdom, Australia, and New Zealand, to share training and resources. Canada provided training fields safely away from the front lines. Pilots were given many hours of classroom and in-flight training.

BELOW: *A flight instructor and his student in front of North American Harvard II airplanes.*

Lloyd Samuel Breadner

During WWII, Breadner turned the RCAF into one of the most powerful air forces in the world. He was at the historic Quebec Conference, which was held on the Plains of Abraham in 1944. King, Roosevelt, and Churchill met there to discuss wartime strategy. After retiring, Breadner was promoted to air chief marshal. He was the first to hold this rank.

ABOVE: *The Canadian government urged people to join the Royal Canadian Air Force to help defeat the Axis powers.*

Harold (Gus) Edwards

A WWI fighter pilot, Edwards entered WWII as group captain. A little over three years later, he was promoted to air marshal. He fought for the right of all Canadians, no matter their race, to be admitted to the forces. He also noticed that Canadian pilots were scattered among many different RAF units. He worked to bring Canadians together into their own **squadrons**.

George (Buzz) Beurling

Beurling was the most successful fighter pilot of World War II. His first few missions were over Europe, but he made his mark in Malta. His **tally** rose to 31 downed enemy planes. He was not unbeatable, though. He was shot down four times over Malta. Each time, he found his way back to his base. He was awarded the Distinguished Flying Medal, the Distinguished Flying Cross, and the Distinguished Service Order in 1942.

ABOVE: *The Distinguished Flying Cross is a medal awarded to those who show valor and bravery while flying in active duty.*

PRIMARY SOURCES

"There are not two ways about it, he was a wonderful pilot and an even better shot."

—BRITISH FLYING ACE JAMES "GINGER" LACEY, ABOUT BEURLING

What do you think?

How did the British Commonwealth Air Training Plan help the Allies?

ABOVE: *The RAF is the oldest air force in the world.*

Britain's Royal Air Force Leaders and Airmen

The Royal Air Force (RAF) is the world's oldest air force. It was founded in 1918. The RAF originally used its planes for strategic bombing. This strategy aims to destroy targets that help an enemy's military operations. Supply lines, factories, bridges, and railways were all targets for bombers. The RAF was **vital** in the Battle of Britain. Its famous Spitfire planes fought the *Luftwaffe* for control of the skies.

Hugh Dowding

As Air Officer Commanding, Hugh Dowding led the fight in the Battle of Britain. Dowding was excellent at managing crews and equipment. He made sure enough pilots were trained. He also made sure airplanes were being built quickly enough to replace damaged or downed planes.

Dowding did not always get along with other senior officers. They thought he was stubborn and stuffy. His troops had a different view. They knew him as truly caring, and felt his decisions were in their best interests.

Douglas Bader

The RAF's most famous flying ace was Douglas Bader. He joined the RAF in 1928 and learned to fly. Three years later, he crashed while doing **aerobatics**. He lost both his legs in the accident, but Bader had a strong will. Only six months later, he had learned to walk on artificial legs without a cane. He also qualified to fly again for the RAF.

When war broke out, Bader took part in several battles including the Battle of Britain. He had 20 confirmed downed planes. In August 1941, his plane was hit and he **bailed out** over Germany. He was taken as a prisoner of war (POW). As soon as he could, he tried to escape. He succeeded but was recaptured many times. He tried to be as much of a pest for the Germans as he could. He finally returned home after his prison camp was liberated in 1945.

What Do You Know?

When Douglas Bader bailed out of his Spitfire, the strap holding his artificial right leg broke. The leg was found in the plane wreckage, but it needed to be repaired. Officers in Britain got word that he had been captured and that his right leg had been damaged. The RAF dropped a replacement leg into enemy territory by parachute.

RIGHT: *Squadron Leader Douglas Bader sits atop his Hawker Hurricane in 1940.*

CHAPTER 5

KEY NAVAL LEADERS IN WWII

AXIS NAVAL LEADERS IN WWII

The sea battles in WWII were the longest and largest in history. Naval leaders had to plan, strategize, and react quickly. In the Atlantic, the German submarines caused chaos for Allied forces by sinking ships and stopping the passage of supplies and troops. In the Pacific, Allied victories over Japan helped to turn the tide of war.

Germany's Naval Leaders in WWII

The *Kriegsmarine* was the German navy. It focused on building a fleet of submarines, called U-boats. The *Kriegsmarine* had more than 1,100 U-boats. They hunted in packs and targeted supply routes.

ABOVE: *The* Kriegsmarine *had more than 1,100 German U-boats at the beginning of WWII.*

RIGHT: *The Nuremberg trials were court trials held after WWII during which the Allies prosecuted German leaders for war crimes.*

Erich Raeder

In 1939, Raeder was named grand admiral—the highest rank in the German navy.

He was not happy that Germany was at war, though. Hitler had told him that he had until 1944 to prepare the navy for war. He did not feel they were ready to take on the powerful Royal Navy, nor that they had time to build enough battleships and destroyers. Hitler told Raeder to focus on the fleet of U-boats instead.

Raeder was good at strategy, but the navy suffered big losses and Hitler lost faith in him. Raeder resigned in 1943. After the war, he was sentenced to life in prison at the Nuremberg trials.

Karl Doenitz

Doenitz began the war as rear admiral. He was in charge of Operation Drumbeat. This was a plan to attack shipping along the east coast of the United States. It used a tactic called "wolfpack," in which U-boats attacked together, like a pack of wolves.

Doenitz was concerned when the Allies began to find and sink many of the U-boats. He suspected spies had broken the secret code the navy used. It was called the "enigma code." He decided to switch to a new, harder version called "Triton." It took Allied code breakers 10 months to break the new code.

In 1943, Doenitz took over as grand admiral after Erich Raeder resigned. It was the beginning of the end of the *Kriegsmarine*. It was losing ships faster than it could replace them. After Hitler's death, Doenitz became president. He made a deal for German soldiers to surrender to the British or Americans, not the Soviets. He worried the Soviets would seek revenge on the Germans.

ABOVE: *Japanese naval officers.*

Japan's Naval Leaders

During the first few months of WWII, the Imperial Japanese Navy (IJL) was very successful. Planes launched from aircraft carriers sank Allied battleships. A **strike force** in the Indian Ocean forced the Allies to retreat. But the Imperial Navy didn't have enough ships and submarines, which eventually led to its defeat.

Isoroku Yamamoto

In 1940, Yamamoto was promoted to admiral. He was told to create a plan to weaken the U.S. Navy. He did not want to go to war with the United States. He thought the IJL would become much stronger over time, but his commanders insisted. Yamamoto's plan was to strike the fleet docked at Pearl Harbor. After that success, he became very confident. He attacked more Allied ports in the South Pacific.

His next target was the small island of Midway. He wanted to finish off the rest of the American ships, which were **stationed** there. The mission was a disaster. The Japanese fleet lost four ships, and Yamamoto was blamed for the defeat.

American code breakers learned that Admiral Yamamoto was going to visit troops. U.S. fighter jets fired on his plane. Yamamoto's plane crashed on the Solomon Islands. Colonel Rex T. Barber fired the shot that killed Yamamoto.

What Do You Know?

The Japanese found Yamamoto's body in the jungle. The Allies had to explain how they knew Yamamoto was on the plane, but they did not want the Japanese to know they had broken their code. American newspapers printed a report that soldiers had seen Yamamoto board the plane. The Japanese Navy believed the story. They didn't change their code.

Chuichi Nagumo

Nagumo was named commander in chief of the navy's aircraft carrier fleet in 1941. He was successful in attacking Allied ships. Until the Battle of Midway, his tally included dozens of enemy ships and more than 100 enemy aircraft. His losses were only a few dozen Japanese pilots.

The Battle of Midway changed everything. The loss of ships, crew, and mechanics affected later battles, and Nagumo resigned as commander-in-chief. He watched as Japan faced defeat. He committed suicide on July 6, 1944.

BELOW: *U.S. Army's Signals Intelligence Service code breakers at work.*

ALLIED NAVAL LEADERS IN WWII

There were big changes in how battles were fought at sea in WWII. U-boats stalked the oceans. Navies used planes launched from aircraft carriers to reach enemy troops and bases.

U.S. Naval Leaders in WWII

In the years before WWII, the United States had a powerful navy. But the U.S. lost its main battleship fleet during the Japanese attack on Pearl Harbor. Luckily for U.S. forces, the aircraft carriers were not damaged.

As the navy rebuilt its fleet, the leaders decided to change the navy's focus. The navy would now mainly use planes **deployed** from the carriers in battles. This new type of naval warfare was very successful.

Ernest King

King was commander-in-chief of the United States fleet during WWII. He was a strong leader who never backed down. After the attack on Pearl Harbor, he didn't want to simply defend against the Japanese. He planned to attack the Japanese in the Pacific. It was a daring move, but it worked.

BELOW: *An Allied warship firing toward the beaches of Normandy.*

ABOVE: *This is what the U.S. naval base at Pearl Habor looked like before the Japanese attacked.*

BELOW: *After the Japanese attack, soldiers worked hard to save lives and ships.*

Royal E. Ingersoll

In 1942, Ingersoll was named commander-in-chief of the Atlantic fleet. He knew that U-boats were a huge problem for the Allied forces. He spoke with commanders stationed along the east coast of the United States. With the information he gathered, he was better able to attack or avoid the U-boat threat. His fleet **escorted** troops and supplies through the dangerous waters from the United Kingdom to the Mediterranean.

Chester W. Nimitz

Nimitz was made commander-in-chief of the Pacific fleet in 1942. His strength was strategizing. He knew how and where to move his troops to best fight the Axis powers. His leadership helped with the victories in the Battles of the Coral Sea and Midway.

Holland Smith

General Smith was commander of the First Marine Division. He trained his men in amphibious (both land and water) warfare, which is an attack from a beach landing. Troops, materials, and vehicles had to move from ships to land quickly. Fast patrol boats called Zodiacs and even mini-submarines were used. This type of warfare was successful in the Pacific. Important islands such as Iwo Jima were recaptured from the Japanese.

What do you think?

Do you think the United States would have entered WWII if the Japanese had not attacked Pearl Harbor? Why or why not?

Britain's Naval Leaders in WWII

At the start of World War II, the British Royal Navy was the largest in the world. The Royal Navy was powerful in surface battles, but it was not ready for a sea battle fought mostly with U-boats.

ABOVE: *The SS* Athenia *was the first ship to be torpedoed by a German U-boat in WWII.*

Sir Alfred Pound

Pound was named First Sea Lord in 1939. One month later, he was promoted to admiral of the fleet, which is the highest rank in the British navy. His leadership helped the Allies win the longest battle of WWII: the Battle of the Atlantic. Pound resigned in 1943 because of poor health. He died just one month later.

Andrew Cunningham

Cunningham was made commander-in-chief one day before he arrived in the Mediterranean. He was in charge of the safety of Allied **convoys**. He knew the main threat was the Italian navy. Cunningham planned an attack on Italian ships at anchor in the harbor of Taranto. This attack marked the beginning of a change in naval warfare. Planes launched from ships became more important than big guns.

Canada's Naval Leaders in WWII

The Canadian navy played a critical role in the Battle of the Atlantic. It supplied Britain with food and materials. The merchant ships carrying these supplies were targeted by the *Kriegsmarine*.

LEFT: *HMS* Arnprior *was a Canadian ship that served as a convoy escort (guard) in the Atlantic Ocean during WWII.*

Leonard W. Murray

When the war began, Murray helped build up Canada's navy. In 1941, Murray was promoted to commodore. He was put in charge of the Newfoundland Escort Force. Destroyers, **corvettes**, and sloops escorted convoys from St. John's, Newfoundland, to Iceland. Once the Newfoundland Escort Force arrived, the British ships would then escort the convoys to England.

BELOW: *HMCS* Saguenay *was a destroyer that served in the Royal Canadian Navy during WWII.*

Harry G. DeWolf

DeWolf was first assigned as the commanding officer of the HMCS *St. Laurent*. This destroyer was sent to the English Channel in 1940. There, DeWolf helped rescue British soldiers who had been stranded on the beaches of Dunkirk, France.

In 1943, DeWolf took command of the HMCS *Haida*. It was called the "fightingest ship in the Royal Canadian Navy." DeWolf kept the English Channel clear of German ships and U-boats. The *Haida* sank 14 enemy ships in just over one year.

KEY ALLIED CODE TALKERS AND CODE BREAKERS

Making and Breaking Codes

Details about an enemy's troops, weapons, and plans were vital in knowing how, when, and where to attack. Both sides used codes to communicate with their commanders and soldiers. These codes kept their plans secret from enemies. The men and women who created codes and learned to decipher enemy codes played a key role in winning battles.

ABOVE: *During WWII German secret codes were decrypted here at Bletchley Park in England.*

Charles Chibitty

ABOVE: *In 2002, Chibbity said, "My language helped win the war, and that makes me proud. Very proud."*

Chibitty was a member of the Native American Comanche tribe. They spoke a rare and unique language. The army knew that a code built on this language would be almost impossible to break. Chibitty was a code talker with the Fourth Infantry Division, and with them he survived the Invasion of Normandy. He was awarded the Victory Medal for his work.

Alan Turing

ABOVE: *Alan Turing was a mathematician and computer scientist who built a machine that could break the secret Nazi codes.*

The Germans had created a very powerful coding machine. It was called the "Enigma Machine." The Nazis used this machine to encode their messages. Alan Turing was a **cryptologist**. He studied and also broke codes. With the help of a team of mathematicians, Turing designed a device that could break the Enigma code. The messages that were decoded helped the Allies win the war.

FURTHER READING AND WEBSITES

BOOKS

Adams, Simon. *DK Eyewitness Books: World War II*. DK Children, 2014.

Bartoletti, Susan Campbell. *Hitler Youth: Growing Up in Hitler's Shadow*. Scholastic, 2005.

Bascomb, Neal. *The Nazi Hunters: How a Team of Spies and Survivors Captured the World's Most Notorious Nazi*. Arthur A. Levine Books, 2013.

Burgan, Michael. *World War II Pilots: An Interactive History Adventure*. Capstone Press, 2013.

Feinberg, Barbara Silberdick. *Douglas MacArthur: American Hero*. Franklin Watts, 1999.

Giblin, James Cross. *The Life and Death of Adolf Hitler*. Clarion Books, 2002.

Gottfried, Ted. *Eleanor Roosevelt: First Lady of the 20th Century*. Franklin Watts, 1997.

Jeffrey, Gary. *Graphic Modern History: World War II, War in the Pacific*. Crabtree Publishing, 2012

McCollum, Sean. *Joseph Stalin* (Wicked History). Franklin Watts, 2010.

WEBSITES

Facts for Kids on Hitler:
http://factsforkids.net/adolf-hitler-facts-kids-rare-facts-adolf-hitler/

Political Leaders of World War II:
http://www.historylearningsite.co.uk/political_leaders_of_world_war_t.htm

Winston Churchill at the BBC:
http://www.bbc.co.uk/schools/primaryhistory/famouspeople/winston_churchill/

World War II at Ducksters:
http://www.ducksters.com/history/world_war_ii/

World War II Facts at Kidskonnect:
https://kidskonnect.com/history/world-war-ii/

AUTHOR BIOGRAPHY

Natalie Hyde is the author of more than 45 fiction and non-fiction books for children. Her non-fiction books cover topics as diverse as genetics, rocks, population patterns, nature, and history. Natalie lives in Southwestern Ontario with her family.

GLOSSARY

ace a pilot who shoots down five or more enemy planes

aerobatics showy flying performance with loops and flips

ammunition bullets and shells for guns

appeasement the act of pleasing someone by giving them what they want

bailed out jumped out of a damaged aircraft

barbarians people who were thought to have no culture or education

brutal extremely cruel

charismatic able to attract people's attention and be very likeable

Commonwealth states that belonged to the British Empire

communism a social and economic system founded on the idea that society as a whole, through its government, should own resources and businesses; results in a large, strong government

conscription the act of forcing people to join the armed forces

convoys groups of ships traveling together

corvettes warships with one tier of guns each

cryptologist a person who uses math and computer codes to turn words into secret messages and vice versa

cyanide a chemical compound that is poisonous

DAP short for Deutsche Arbeiterpartei

D-Day June 6, 1944—the day the Allies began their campaign to free Europe from Nazi control

death camp a prison camp where many are put to death

democracy a system of government in which citizens have a voice, either directly or through representatives

deployed moved into position for military action

dictatorship a form of government in which citizens are ruled by someone with total power

dogfights fights in the air between two planes

dominated controlled completely

dominion a territory of another country

economic referring to the income and wealth of a country

emigrate to leave one country to live in another

escort to follow and protect

executed put to death according to a death sentence

feudal belonging to a social system from long ago, in which people worked and fought for a lord in return for protection and land

figurehead a leader without real power

firing squad a military group ordered to shoot a person sentenced to death

First Lord of the Admiralty department of British government that had control over naval affairs

Holocaust the murder of millions of Jewish people during WWII

integrated allowing all races of people to be included

internment the imprisonment of people without a trial

invasion an attack by a large number of soldiers

kamikaze a plane loaded with explosives for a suicide attack

NATO short for North Atlantic Treaty Organization; an organization created after WWII to provide security for all member countries

neutral not involved and not supporting one side or the other

Nuremberg trials trials held after WWII, during which the Allies prosecuted German leaders for war crimes

occupy to take possession of

pact a formal agreement between countries

radar a system used to detect moving objects

raid a sudden attack

recruit to enlist someone in the armed forces

squadrons divisions of two or more troops

stationed assigned to a certain place

strategy a plan for military operations during a war or battle

strike force a military group organized for a sudden attack

surrender give up

tactic a careful plan for battle

tally score

technology scientific knowledge

trade barriers rules that make it easier to buy local rather than imported products

Tripartite Act the military agreement signed between Germany, Italy, and Japan

vital absolutely necessary

INDEX